GOSPEL-FOCUSED
HUSBANDS

GOSPEL-FOCUSED HUSBANDS

How Do I Love My Wife as Christ Loved the Church?

David A. Coats

Gospel-Focused Husbands
How do I love my wife as Christ loved the Church?

David A. Coats

Copyright © 2022 David A. Coats
www.coatscounsel.net

ISBN: 9798417719684

Cover design and typeset by www.greatwriting.org

Gospel-focused Husbands 6

Gospel Love: A Self-sacrificial, Active Choice....................... 12

The Gospel and the Union Between the Husband and Wife... 18

Gospel Sex: Loving my Wife as Christ Loved the Church....... 24

The Gospel and Husbands Who Struggle 28

The Gospel in Loving, Servant-Leader Husbands 32

Conclusion.. 40

Final Questions & Homework.. 44

Other Resources for Husbands 47

Other books by Dave & Judi Coats 47

Gospel-focused Husbands

· ·

*Husbands can love their wives as Christ loved
the Church and gave himself for it (Ephesians 5:25)*

Joel came into a counseling session with an anger problem. At least that is what he thought his problem was. But after meeting for some weeks and identifying what was in his heart, he admitted, "I don't like it. My dad was always giving my mom her choices. He lived like she should get what she wanted. I'm tired of never having my way in life." He didn't recognize that the gospel calls him to love his wife.

Tim, another counselee, explained that every time that he and his wife had a fight, the argument centered around things they differed on; and she never gave him the respect he deserved. *He wasn't going to put up with it.* So he blasted her. Tim didn't know what gospel love for his wife looks like.

What should God witness as we interact with our wives? What should God see in our hearts? What kinds of prayers should God hear from us as we seek to be the kinds of husbands God has called us to be? I hope that this short study will help answer some of those questions. I want to put practical meat on the bones of the text that Paul delivers to husbands in Ephesians 5.

Have you heard this set of statements from the New Testament?

- Men, "*love your wife*" as Christ loved the church (Ephesians 5:25).
- Men, "*love your neighbor.*" Your wife is your closest neighbor (Matthew 22:39).
- Men, you are to "*love one another*" in the body, the

Church. Thirteen times we as men are commanded to love others in the church body.

- Men, *"love your enemy."* If your wife is not in the body, then you still have to love her like Christ loved those who were his enemies (Matthew 5:44).
- Men, *"do unto others"* as you would have others do to you if you were a mess (Luke 6:31).

The point of the preceding statements is that we have no "out" or reason for not loving the woman we are married to, the woman we are living with every day of our lives. But we don't need all of those other commands. The first one that Paul gives us is the call *to live out the gospel* with our wives every day. We have heard plenty about the gospel in the last two decades and more.

Here is what I mean by the gospel. Humans rebelled against God in Eden when they had everything they needed. Instead of destroying them, God promised rescue from the terrible effects of their sin against Him. God would provide someone to take their place. Jesus was and is our rescuer, our sin-substitute, who paid for our sin.

It is this good news that we need to constantly be called back to in Christ. It is the gospel that should motivate us to live for God (2 Corinthians 5:9–13). We are to be driven by the love of God that he fleshed out *for us.* If we do reflect the gospel in our daily lives, I believe our wives will see the gospel on display through our words, responses, attitudes, actions, and reactions to them.

That parallel between how Christ, the Son of God, loved us, His church, and the way a husband is to love his wife—that parallel is what I want us to see in this study. This is our opportunity to live out the good news in our marriage. I have taken on the admonition God has given to me that I must follow Christ in my home, and I hope to encourage you to do the same in your home.

If husbands can continue to preach the gospel to themselves daily, this practice will greatly help them to love their wives as Christ did the church; and it will help their wives to be called to respond to their husbands as the church responds to Christ. Let's turn to a few illustrations.

This self-denial is the kind of gospel husbands are called to. It is not about if you feel "in love." Instead it is about acting based on the call of God in the gospel. God didn't feel "in love" with us. He loved us when we were sinners. Here is the gospel: God loves us in this kind of self-sacrificial way.

- He died *for us* while we were his enemies and in opposition to His kingdom (Ephesians 2:1–4; Romans 5:8). *Are you willing to sacrifice for your wife in this kind of way?*
- We were people that wanted our own way, like sheep that go astray (Isaiah 53:6). *Can you pursue your wife and care for her even if she is going her own way?*
- We did not want God, His ways, His thoughts, or His plan (Romans 3:10–12). Maybe your wife is on her way out of the relationship with you? She thinks only of herself. *This is your opportunity to show her what God did when he came to earth.*
- We wanted to be at the center of our life and thoughts and plans. God chose to love us, and on the basis of that love, He died *for us*. How should we love Him? We love Him because He first loved us. *So love your wife that way. Love her and do things for her as Christ did for you.*

What about your author, Dave Coats? I don't see myself as living this command out well. I have had the privilege of living with my wife Judi since we said "I do" in August of 1979. I was idealistic about this marriage. I saw us as a young couple that would get to serve God together. What I *did not* see was how proud and self-centered I was as a man and husband. We went to Haiti as missionaries where God began to break down my pride and humble me as a husband. He showed me how little I knew about living out the gospel with my wife. God used some deep waters in Haiti, including a time where God nearly took my wife home to heaven, followed by her struggle with depression, to expose my self-centered life. I was way over my head spiritually, but at least I knew how to cry out to God for help.

- I would say that in the last ten years especially that God has been working on this particular arena of my life.
- What do I think of when she is sick?
- How do I act when she has a difficult day?
- Do I demand sex when she is exhausted?
- What are my motives when she needs me to take extra time to listen and to hear what she has to say?
- What kind of words do I form in my thoughts and what kinds of desires and feelings do I experience in my heart?
- How well do I hear her and how well do I show compassion to her?
- How easy is it for me to be defensive and proud?
- How do I pitch in and help?
- Do I put her needs first?

Have I wanted to be done with my marriage? *No. Never.* But have I been like Christ, ready to show love, express love, live out godly love, and patiently care for my wife by walking in the Spirit? No. Can I truly say I have lived out the gospel of Christ towards Judi? Am I like Christ, ready to share in my wife's weaknesses? No. Maybe grudgingly. Christ came to this earth in order to let us know he cares. Often times for me, I respond with an inner spirit that is complaining to itself. And then I repent and ask God to daily change me into a servant-leader-lover of my wife as Christ did for the church.

Think about how Jesus came in human form so we would know what God was like and how much he cared for us personally. Now Jesus is in heaven, but *every believing husband has the opportunity to show our wives just a little bit of what Jesus is like and what he did in the gospel.* I know that sounds like a high ideal, but apparently this was God's idea that we love our wives in the way Jesus does the church. Living the gospel is another way the "cross-centered" life shows up in very normal street clothes for my wife to get a little glimpse of Jesus.

- God's love was evident as Jesus did miracles but also chose to limit himself within a human body so we would know Him and be known by Him. What ways do I sacrifice and limit myself from what I might do or have so that my wife can know love and experience God?
- Jesus loves us through his praying, mediating, hearing us, and directing us. Can a husband pray and hear and help and direct his wife in a caring and considerate fashion?
- He loves us enough to comfort us. Will we comfort our wives? Will we know how to do that?
- His love is shown in how much he knows us and wills to make us more like Him. Do we know our wives well enough and express our desire for them to be like Christ?
- Because of his creative work and because of his cross work, God loves us in intimate, specific, and individual ways as He knows everything about us. Our emotional, spiritual, physical, social, sexual, and intellectual being is fully known by God. Husband, bring the gospel home to your wife. Love her in intimate, specific ways that reflect her emotional, spiritual, physical, sexual, social, and intellectual being.

1

Gospel Love: A Self-sacrificial, Active Choice

· · · · · · · · · ·

Can we envision love as God defines it and as God shows love to us? Love is the kind of activity and choice that is selfless. This kind of love is the opposite of self-centered living. And I will admit it. I struggle greatly with life being all about me. His divine kind of love refuses to put me first. God's kind of love chooses to be others-focused and begins with the one person in our life that will see and experience our love the most. Even when the husband is good or does good, it still might not be God's kind of love, especially if it is self-focused and driven to get something in return.

The opposite of self-sacrificial love is taking from a person. That selfish kind of love is manipulative, doing to them or for them so we can get something back. Being a "giver" is *God's essence,* and giving is what *God does.* Apparently, husbands need to hear this repeatedly. I can see how much I need the repetition.

Maybe we just don't know this love at all. Maybe we don't understand God's love. We have been bombarded with "my needs being met" teaching. Maybe, and most likely, we don't very easily change how we interact with our wives. From my own life, I know my need to hear about God's love repeatedly is because I am so naturally self-centered. Three times in this Ephesians passage Paul says to the husbands that they are to love their wives (Ephesians 5:25, 28, 33).

God wants to see the gospel acted out in this relationship between the husband and the wife. It is like a gospel play lived out on the stage of life. We get to see what Christ has done and what he is doing based on his love. Then his love comes alive in us as we live out life with pure motives.

- The gospel says that Jesus loved sinners in their worst case. They were not desirable (Romans 5:5–11). Do we think we are an exception?
- The gospel tells us that sinners needed God to love them and act on their behalf (Ephesians 2:1–10). There was nothing sinners could do to "attract" God's love to them.
- The gospel reminds us that sinners could not have done for themselves what only God could do and what Jesus did for them (Ephesians 2:6–9). We should be so overwhelmed by this godly love.
- The gospel points out to us how Jesus came to help us and what his goal was. In this same way, God loved the world (John 1:12; 3:16). He wants us to be family so we can become more like our heavenly Father every day.
- The gospel is motivated in love to bring mercy, grace, and hope into our lives (Ephesians 2 and Colossians 3). Imagine life without Jesus and the impact of His love – where would we be?

So how should this kind of gospel living show up in my life on behalf of my wife?

- What are the worst case scenarios that a husband will experience with his wife? She may be tired and emotional and not acting or talking reasonably. Will I care for her? Will I be patient with her?
- She may blame her husband for things that are not under his control. She may fear things that seem common place or she may fear things that are not likely to ever happen. Will he help her?
- She may have doubts about his faithfulness even if he hasn't shown himself unfaithful. She will experience emotional ups and downs because of her monthly cycle or because of pregnancy or perhaps in post-partum peri-

ods. Will he embrace her weakness and let her know she is no less loved because of this struggle?

- She may become deathly sick or suffer an illness that will be debilitating over time. Will I give of myself when I could do other things with my life and I could spend my time with others?
- She may struggle in her faith and wrestle with seeing God in the realities of a sinful world. She may allow doubts to cloud her mind and attack her heart. Will I encourage her faith and gently point her to Christ, the one who is our Hope?
- She may fall prey to jealousy. Will I react in anger or will I be patient as Christ is with His church?
- She could struggle with a myriad of other things that are common or uncommon. Will I love her and live out the gospel and respond to her like Christ did with the church?
- What are some ways I need to act on my wife's behalf? She may go through struggles with her family or with my family where they are not loving and kind. But I am to love her and to let her know we are united and together in this journey of faith.
- She may have to deal with people in the church that are sinful or judging and act in unchristian ways towards her. She may feel inferior to others around her. She may feel like she doesn't fit in or is just not connected to those around her. But I am to let her know I don't judge her and that she is accepted in Christ and with me always.
- She may struggle with the financial picture and the seemingly unending and unexpected bills that are not in the budget. I must give her confidence that we will do our best and also that we will trust God to help us resolve these financial hardships by God's grace (Proverbs 3:5–6).
- What are some things that my wife just can't do for herself? Can I imagine what it is like for God to look down at his church and see our puny efforts and struggles? How does Jesus love us in these times? He walks with us. We never feel like we are a bother to God.

- What is God's design for my wife and how can I help love her to that design? His design for my wife is that she would become more like Jesus. God made her to know him and love him and enjoy him forever.

God created her in a way that she can respond to him and experience his love in her life personally, not just corporately as part of the church. She is to know this reality now and progress in that walk with God through our life together.

But unless I am thinking about and talking about how she is growing in knowing and loving God and becoming more like Christ, she will feel like she is on her own. Do I talk about her walk with God? Do I pray through scripture with her?

If not, she will feel like it is just men that have the inside track with God and the Spirit. I need to want her to flourish in Christ and grow in her theology in this pursuit of God. I need to be aware of her understanding of God and her thinking and responding to what God has done. This is good news for every wife.

Do I just come home from work, expect food to be ready, and head to watch ESPN? Or if she works as well, do I assume she will figure it out – food prep, laundry, bills, cleaning?

Do I sit down in my chair and ignore the kids while she has to deal with their complaining and fighting? Do I ever ask her if she has time to read and pray? Do I provide that time for her?

How can I help my wife experience mercy, grace, and hope? If she is to know the gospel in action it will be through my self-sacrificial responses, words, and concerns for her. She will know she wasn't always thinking or speaking biblically, but I want her to know God's grace and hope. When I could be judgmental, I instead need to show mercy and grace as Christ does to me.

How do I love my wife as Christ loved the Church?

2

The Gospel and the Union Between the Husband and Wife

· · · · · · · · · · · · · · · · ·

The New Testament tells us that something happens as a result of our new life in Christ. The good news is that when we are regenerated and placed as "sons" of God, we are now "one" or united with God in Christ (1 Corinthians 12:13). We are a part of His Body, which is the Church (Ephesians 4:11–16).

This concept of unity is to be reflected in the relationship between the husband and wife (Ephesians 5:31–33). When you read this section of Ephesians by Paul, you need to see what he is saying about marriage and the reflection of God in us from the day we say our vows. It is a picture of God's love and what He has done to make us one in Him. We are united to God with the Father and the Son (John 17:20-23). He loves and cares for his bride, the Church, as a part of himself.

- The gospel brought us into a relationship with God so that we are made one "in Christ," so God knows and cares for us in every way as our pain and hurt pushes in on our soul.
- *My wife and I are two sinners united before God* in a relationship before God that demands that we love one another, knowing that the other person has been called to reciprocate love, too, as a sinner. You are called to love your wife like Christ did all sinners, and she is to submit to a sinner as you lead and love her. Matthew 7:1-4 shows that we must begin with confession and repentance in our own hearts.
- Unity or closeness means "one-flesh" and is a reminder

of what I do for my own body. It is as if I am to treat my wife's body as my body, her concerns are my concerns. We are to be so close as to be one. This unity or oneness is more than sexual. It is spiritual and emotional. In fact, these three are all entwined. I am to feel what she feels and to be so close to her that I know what is going on inside her soul as much as possible.

This too is a part of the "good news" to a wife. Her husband wants to be close to her and know her intimately. So what do I do, how do I listen, and how do I work to understand her struggles? She is mine and I am hers. We are one. There is to be a unity of purpose, desires, and plans that are shared in all things. I am convinced that the word *shared* is a huge biblical concept that the world doesn't understand. But marriage before God is not just two people living together in some kind of a partnership that is like a good and productive business relationship, holding onto my "stuff." In contrast, I am to be *all in* on this relationship with my wife.

At times some "Christian" psychology or other kinds of counseling picture men and women as so different that they can't really understand each other. So then this kind of love of husbands for wives isn't possible. Is it a struggle? Yes. Does it take time and investment? Yes. That definitely sounds like sacrificial love as defined by God.

We share ALL things in life. This is unity and oneness. The more that we share, the more that we care. I care for her and all that affects or touches her. And in turn, she will learn to care and share in my life.

- *Don't blame her.* Love her. Clear your heart of your sin struggle, especially your pride. Then continue to love her sacrificially and humbly. Seek her good in the gospel. Find ways to resolve things in your heart and hers. Everything that hurts my wife, should hurt me and the same for my wife. We are touched by what touches each other.
- What kind of love do I have for my wife and how does it

compare to the way I love myself? I would suppose that this biblical oneness pictures the closest you can be to me without being me. We are sharing life together in many ways.

- List them. How do you share in her life and how does she share in yours? Discuss the following categories: financial, purpose, goals, plans, joys, sorrows, success, failures, house and property, investments, future life, work and immediate tasks. How do you share together in them?
- Do I seek to provide for, care for, and think in advance about my wife's life as I do for myself? If I do a good job of that, it would certainly be good news to my wife if I cared this much.
- Think on what it means to be "one" or in a union of the closest personal, human level. You can't be split and going your own ways. You are a team. You can't be competing between you. That is a recipe for disaster and failure. And there is more good news here!

I know. Judi and I have always been "competitive" in games. It is fun. Most of the time (especially when I win). What is going on in my heart? I want that edge. My old man in my heart is struggling with finding a way to enjoy seeing her win. Not only do I want to win, but it seems like I want to push her down as I win.

Really? What God is explaining in oneness is that I am hurting myself because she is part of me. We are one. Whenever I pursue selfishness or think selfishly, I am not loving her.

- Think about the last time you made choices and decisions based on what was best for you.
- Remind yourself that every financial decision and every planning choice you make affects her. She should be in on all those decisions.
- Consider the last time you did something without even thinking about how she would feel.

- What does it say about her when you just ignore her input? She is one with you. The gospel calls you to ask her how she is feeling and thinking about the decision you are making. That is good news. Jesus knows what is best for his church. Do you know what is best for your wife in this situation?
- Did you buy the car you wanted the most?
- Did you choose the house based on your priorities and what was most important to you? What kinds of things matter to her? Do you even know? Can you make a short list?
- Did you plan your vacation based on what you would most enjoy? Is your wife supposed to just be happy for you and hang out for the next week?
- Do you even know what it is to enjoy what she does in leisure and in work?
- Did you put your family through hardships when you made the last big purchase?
- When you forgot to pay the bank on time or neglected to follow through on a particular needed upkeep on a vehicle or appliance, did you consider how your wife would have to deal with it as well. She is emotionally and spiritually joined to you, and everything you do impacts her.

How do I love my wife as Christ loved the Church?

3

Gospel Sex: Loving my Wife as Christ Loved the Church and Sacrificed Himself for the Church

· · · · · · · · · · · · · · · · · · · ·

Now this may be news to some of you husbands, but sex is not just about you. God made sex as a mutually enjoyable activity that reflects the goodness and greatness of God in his creation plan. It is beautiful, and it is to reflect God.

In fact, I have heard it said to women that if they don't meet their husband's need in sex, then their husband may turn elsewhere. Bad teaching. It is the blame game. What a horrible weight for the wife to carry! Where did you find that in your Bible?

Husband, you are to sacrifice yourself and your drives and put your wife first. Christ put the church and her greatest need above all else. He put his love on display as he set aside what he could have had in order to provide for and care for us.

In 1 Corinthians 7:1-5, Paul pictures the marriage bed as something mutual. Mutual love in sex is beautiful. But Paul's words show that my wife owns my body and I own hers. So we both get what we desire, right? No. That isn't Paul's point. We are to be focused on the joy and pleasure of our spouse and not our own.

Unfortunately, in most marriages, it isn't a mutual joy. In most marriages, men know what they want and demand it as often and at whatever time they want it. That is not sacrificial love as Christ would live it out with his bride, the church.

- Do you know what your wife struggles with when you want sex?

- Do you know her physical and emotional fears that she can take into bed with you? Do you know how to assure her of your love, regardless of whether you have sex or not?
- Do you know her background and what, if any, baggage she brings into your physical intimacy?
- Does she know that you care about her despite how well things go in bed? Have you asked her? Do you know what brings her pleasure and helps her feel prized and cherished?
- Do you know her schedule and body fatigue and the demands of her life well enough that you know if she is even physically able to have sex and enjoy it when you desire it? Do you know what time of the day and when during the week is best for her?
- When she is pregnant, have you thought about all that she is experiencing before you move towards sex? Do you even know what her emotions and hormones are going through and how that will affect her in bed? Do you think you understand her discomfort?
- When she has had a hard day with the kids or at her work place, do you think you deserve sex whether she is exhausted or not? Does she feel cornered and in demand for sex or does she freely offer it?
- Have you thought about how Jesus calls you to deny yourself and follow Him? That means if you are going to be like Jesus in the gospel, you will do what it takes to reflect a Christlike character and demeanor. Yes discipleship and following Christ includes the sexual arena of your life as well.
- If you are newly married, are you taking precautions to not hurt her but to be gentle and caring in order to reflect Christ. Have you asked her if what you do feels good and is enjoyable or if what you are doing hurts her physically? Are you able to have such conversations without it being uncomfortable? Work at it.

By the way, I will say this. When I finally came to understand that God's plan for sex was mutual pleasure and that my first thoughts and my main focus was to be towards my wife, it made my pleasure so much different. Unselfish sex leads to a godly expression and enjoyment that truly allows you to experience this God-ordained design in the way he made it to be.

4

The Gospel and Husbands Who Struggle With Loving Their Wives as Christ Loved the Church

• • • • • • • • • • • • • • • • •

Every husband struggles with this command. Every husband is going to fall short of Christ as a husband to the Church. But that is no excuse for not trying. Did you ever try living this way? Did you start and give up?

Remember that we are commanded to live this way with our wives. It isn't a suggestion. Just as the wife is to learn what it means to be in submission to her husband as the leader in the home, so the husband is to learn what it means to love his wife like Christ.

I don't know how many husbands have sat across from me and said they are struggling with how their wife doesn't give them respect. Imagine the number of wives that would say something like this about their husband.

"He doesn't love me like Christ loved the church."
"He doesn't sacrifice for me."
"He is all about himself."
"He doesn't even know me or care about me."

Your failures should not mark the rest of your life as a loving leader. Your Christlike change into a gospel-driven man should be evident every year.

- Set goals for yourself. Plan on how you will get better at living out the gospel of Christ with your wife.
- Ask her to list ways you can be more sacrificial. Are you afraid she will take advantage of you? Join Jesus in that

list. But it is doubtful she will ask too much of you.

- Have quarterly checkup points. Plan to meet with your wife to discuss how you are doing.
- Get *specific*. Don't just choose to wander around in your marriage as a generally good guy that fails in a number of specific ways. List the goals. Look at the suggestions in this mini-book. Highlight the ones that hit home.
- Celebrate progress. Ask your wife to encourage you when you are on target. Let her know you are trying to change how you think, act, and respond to her.
- Start now. Make a list of 10 ways you will care for your wife like Jesus did for the church and work on it every week this year.

5

The Gospel in Loving, Servant-Leader Husbands

• • • • • • • • • • • •

L ove brought the ultimate *"servant leader"* to earth to people who would not understand Him. But he loved them enough to live sacrificially in a way that would be good news once-for-all to them. In Mark 10:35–45, we see what it is like to love and to lead as a servant leader. If I am to love my wife as Christ, I must lead her in love as a servant.

But think for a moment what this meant for Jesus.

- He came to people who didn't want him to come as a servant. They wanted a powerful king to liberate them from Rome.
- He came to people that hated him. They wanted him dead. They would form temporary pacts of unity in order to kill him.
- He had disciples that didn't really understand his mission. They lived with him and saw him at his best every day. Serving people. They still didn't get what Jesus was doing.
- He had to endure the misrepresentation, the misunderstanding, and ultimately the hatred of people for whom he had come to rescue and to die for. There was not anything he would not do to accomplish this mission, including going to a crucifixion death.

In the New Testament world of Mark 7:45, the *diakonos* (noun) or one who *diakoneo* (verb) was one who reached out to others in order to render a service for those who needed it most. It is love-prompted service in ways that are driven by the gospel kindness of God. So it is also assisting others by performing duties that are often humble and menial in nature, including mundane activities (Acts 6:1–3), activities that may seem without dignity (see Proverbs15:3 for how God looks for even the smallest good being done). It seems to be especially connected with personal service. We are *useful* to others by our service. But the service will always be for the benefit of those being served. It is work done for their welfare, especially their spiritual welfare.

It is interesting that in our twenty-first century world, much of the philosophy of our day is focused on what is best "for me." Similarly, the Greek world of the New Testament saw what the writer says of Jesus here as dishonorable. The Greek culture lifted up self as what was best and should be developed. That was the priority. It is not hard to see that being a husband as a servant-leader was not highly prized back then nor is it now. Here are some passages that describe *diakonos* activity.

- Matthew 25:44, The servant was caring for those in prison.
- Acts 6:2, The servant was caring for the physical needs of others.
- 2 Corinthians 9:1, The servant was meeting needs of those who are financially struggling.
- 1 Corinthians 12:5, The servant would do any service offered to others that builds up their faith.
- 1 Peter 4:10–11, The servant was a steward of God's grace (gospel) to others.
- Hebrews 6:10, The servant did works and acts of love for the saints.
-

So we should not lead our family and our wife like the rest of the world of husbands and leaders do. We are not to "lord it over" our wives. We are to lead them as servants. The way Jesus leads His church, we must lead our wives. John 13 shows this love illustrated as Jesus took out a towel and washed the disciples' feet in order that they would know service and remember what he did for them. Do you see the most menial task acted out for our example and learning? How would a husband do this kind of task for his wife?

Jesus wanted all of us who would follow Jesus to see, hear, and almost smell this example. He did not want us to miss how this kind of spiritual work was to be lived out. Nothing was below Him.

So it is with our loving and leading our wives. Be willing to lay down your life, your expectations, your dreams, in order that she would know all that God has for her in you. Nothing related to my wife is out of my domain. Nothing is too low or below me.

- What ways can I "care for" my wife in menial tasks? We should be able to list about fifty or so. I will get you started with a few suggestions.
- What ways can I care for her in the physical realm?
- What ways can I think about and care for her and the impact of financial struggles?
- What ways can I help to point her to Christ in order to help build her faith when she is struggling to trust or see God in life?
- What ways can I help her experience and know God's grace when she doesn't see it?
- What kinds of acts and words and deeds will show how much I am willing to help her?
- What kinds of acts and deeds are menial in daily tasks that she may struggle with or have a hard time completing?
- What kinds of weakness of the body cause her to struggle with keeping up with life?
- What physical touch and encouragement does she enjoy that isn't sexual?
- What ways do I express my appreciation for her?
- How often do I ask her how she is doing and what she would appreciate the most?

- How often do I pray with her and for her while she is listening?
- In what ways do I consider her sexual pleasures and joys ahead of my own?
- Consider examples of menial tasks: dishes, floors, diapers, dusting, reading to kids, helping change sheets, fold clothes, clean toilets, put kids to bed, get kids up, help kids get their clothes on, get kids ready for school, check on school work, help with homework, prepare a meal, clean up after the meal.
- Go to the store with your wife. Take her on errands, just to spend time with her.
- Put together a list of the things that are needed around the house, things generally needed in life. Work on that list. Do something with it.
- If you can't do the projects on the list, hire a teen or a handyman to help you get them done. Find someone from your church that can do them.
- If your wife is sick or has an injury, do you consider all this work that is undone? Do you feel inconvenienced in your heart? What kind of servant are you?

Philippians 2:1–11 is another gospel-packed passage (focused on Christ and his becoming a servant by taking on flesh for our redemption) overflowing with the specific call to live in loving consideration of what is going on in the lives of those closest to us. Be like Jesus. Serve. Be humble. Set aside what you could do or want and focus on the gospel-driven task at hand.

This word for *servant* is different from that of Mark 10:43–45. The *doulos* (Philippians 2:7), or *bond-slave*, is a person in the Roman world that had a particular role. He had no "rights" or privileges. His time was owned by his master. He had no belongings. He was 24/7 a *doulos, bond-slave* in the household.

- How about you as a husband? Do you put yourself at your wife's disposal? Can you turn off the email and the phone

messaging and listen to what she needs of you?
- Do you demand your rights?
- Do you want special privileges as the man in the house? Why? Jesus is the head of all things but he left the adoration of heaven and its throne for the church. He served us with gospel power.
- Do you feel you are owed a certain kind of position or status as the man in the house? You are not God. You are just the husband of your wife and her servant lover.
- What is your attitude as you lead and as you love your wife? Is it Philippians 2 humility?
- What kind of things are you willing to do for her? You are owned by God and belong to your wife.
- Do you have some things in your house that nobody else touches? Are there places that no one else should go? Are these places and things off-limits because they are yours?
- Will you do everything in your power and ability to make life enjoyable for your wife?
- Will you live out the gospel for her every day by the power of God and His grace?

Those at Columbia International University know the story of former President Robertson McQuilkin, who stepped down from his post in order to love and care for his wife, her final ten years being bed ridden. As she went through the stages of Alzheimers (the early part of this story is told in the book *A Promise Kept*), he was loving and caring for his wife. He was living out the gospel before the students, faculty, and administration. Listen to the gospel that resonates here.

It has to do with God's love. No one ever needed me like Muriel, and no one ever responded to my efforts so totally as she. It's the nearest thing I've experienced on a human plane to what my relationship with God was designed to be: God's unfailing love poured out in constant care of helpless me. Surely, he planned that relationship to draw from the kind of love and gratitude Muriel had for her man. Her insatiable – even desperate – longing to be with me, her quiet confidence in my ability and desire to care for her, a mirror of reflection of what my love for God should be. That was the first discovery – the power of love to liberate in the very bondage imposed by unwanted circumstances. People don't always understand that. McQuilkin, *A Promise Kept*, pg. 33 (1998).

How do I love my wife as Christ loved the Church?

Conclusion

• • • • • • • • • • • • •

Think on the gospel. What is encompassed in the gospel? It is God's love; that love has acted towards us.

- God's gospel love is unconditional. Is my love towards my wife based on certain conditions? Do I have a desire to love her in ways that will bring the greatest benefit to her?
- Do I wait to see how she acts towards me before I act in love and care for her? See how God loving us first made it possible for us to love him in return. Think about what we would be like if God did not love us first. Do that for your wife regardless of what emotions or feelings or problems she has. See what it changes.
- God's great love is graciously offered to those who do not deserve it. Does my wife deserve my love? Probably not. But more importantly, does she have to earn it? No. Freely serve her with no strings attached.
- God's love is eternal, freely offered and never rescinded. Are there days I don't feel like living sacrificially? Yes. I am selfish. Those are the days I need to act out God's love. Every day while my wife and I are on this earth united before God, I am to love her this way. I am never to stop loving her as Christ did the church.
- God's love is purposed to bring us back to our original design by God. We are to be like Him. So I have the opportunity to walk alongside my wife in a journey of faith that leads us both to God, to know Him above all.

- God's love is expressed so that we might find our greatest joy in Him. My love is to be lived out and expressed so that my wife will find her greatest joy in her God.
- God's love will bring us to know and to be righteous before God. My love is to help my wife be more righteous daily.
- God's love moved Christ to take our place, the just for the unjust, the righteous for the ungodly, the judge took the place of the guilty and condemned. Do I think that there will be many times that I can step in for her and help her? Yes.
- God showed His love or acted out His love to and for us (Romans 5:8) in a way that was clear and open to the world and specifically evident to us as His own. If people around you that see your marriage were asked to describe your relationship to your wife, what would they say? Would they say that you are a sacrificial person with your wife? Ask a godly mentor this question.
- God acted out his love by taking flesh and sharing in our world and our trouble. Husband, you need to do the same. Share in your wife's world, her troubles, her heart aches and fears. Bear with her struggles of every kind and shape.

Final Questions & Homework

1. What are you going to do now?

2. What are some goals you have set?

3. Who can encourage you along with your wife?

4. How can your small group, life group, missional community (whatever you call it) get involved?

5. What passage are you going to memorize in order to keep this fresh in your mind?

6. How can you highlight this truth and put it in front of you daily?

7. *What would be some immediate homework you can assign yourself:*

    a. I challenge you to highlight just ten of these bullet points in the mini-book.

    b. Now look at them carefully. If it is a question, answer the question specifically. If it is a statement, plan specific ways you will live out that characteristic.

    c. Ask someone in your church to hold you

accountable. Have them ask you for specific follow-through when you talk.

d. Plan one night each week to sit down with your wife and talk about these statements and goals. Ask her input on what a specific quality would look like for her. Ask her how she hopes you will answer the question. Pray with her about these goals.

e. When you finish the first ten, move on to the next five. Don't bite off more than this. Follow through. Ask for God's help daily.

f. Write out these statements or the answers to the questions and make them visible for you to see daily.

g. Take a white board marker and write at the top of your mirror, "Love your wife AS Christ loved the church." [I promise that as long as you don't use permanent marker it will wipe off. Although some of us may need it as a permanent reminder.]

h. Depend on the Spirit to help you live out the gospel with your wife. So ask for his help daily.

Other Resources for Husbands

Rob Green, *Not Tonight Honey.*
Lou Priolo, *The Complete Husband.*
Lou Priolo, *Selfishness: From Loving Yourself to Loving Your Neighbor.*
Stuart Scott, *Biblical Manhood.*
Stuart Scott, *The Exemplary Husband.*
Stuart Scott, *From Pride to Humility.*
Stuart Scott, *Communication and Conflict Resolution.*
John Street. *Men Counseling Men.*
Ed Wheat, *Intended for Pleasure.*

Other books by Dave & Judi Coats

Dave Coats, *Soul Purity: A Workbook for Counselors and Small Groups*
Dave & Judi Coats, *Help! My Teen is Rebellious*
Dave & Judi Coats, *Choosing Wisdom: Solomon's Proverbs Reclaimed*
Judi Coats, *A Sentence Diagramming Primer: The Reed & Kellogg System Step-By-Step*

The apostle Paul's words in Ephesians 5 have always been a challenge to husbands throughout the ages. He sets the bar high—we are to love our wives "as Christ loved the church and gave himself for her"—and that is huge. So loving our wives is not a phrase to be ignored. In fact, we could say that the gospel is in full view in this passage. The good news for wives should be experienced not only in what Christ did on the cross but in their husbands' lives on a daily basis. Although it is true that Ephesians 5 has been preached and often this text has been mentioned, perhaps for the first time husbands will have in their hands a practical guide, based on the gospel of God, how to live out this command.

This little book has already been a great help to counselors, pastors, and the men they want to help to please God and to help reflect his character in the way they lead and love their wives.

Dr. Dave Coats is a certified counselor with ACBC and loves to see how God uses the Word to address people's problems. He has also taught biblical counseling in three different countries and has led a counseling program at the university level.

Author website: www.Coatscounsel.net

Made in the USA
Middletown, DE
05 September 2022

72290517R00029